THE CLASSIC SAAB 900

Richard Horner

AMBERLEY

In loving memory of Derek and Betty Horner.

Front Cover image: Courtesy of Valmet Automotive.
Back Cover image: Courtesy of *Practical Classics*/Jason Critchell.

First published 2016

Amberley Publishing
The Hill, Stroud
Gloucestershire, GL5 4EP

www.amberley-books.com

Copyright © Richard Horner, 2016

The right of Richard Horner to be identified as the
Author of this work has been asserted in
accordance with the Copyrights, Designs and
Patents Act 1988.

ISBN 978 1 4456 5373 0 (print)
ISBN 978 1 4456 5374 7 (ebook)

British Library Cataloguing in Publication Data.
A catalogue record for this book is available from
the British Library.

Typeset in 10pt on 13pt Celeste.
Typesetting by Amberley Publishing.
Printed in the UK.

Contents

Introduction

The classic Saab 900, produced only from 1978 to 1993, was a unique car that brought together the very best in Scandinavian design flair, practical thinking, advanced engineering and safety. This stylish and supremely accomplished compact executive car was Saab's most successful model ever, with more than 908,000 vehicles sold across the world. It is so iconic that, when people think of Saab the car maker, the classic 900 is invariably the model that comes to mind.

Its long production run is testimony to its success, as is the cult status that modern classic-car enthusiasts have bestowed upon it. Across Europe and the US, a number of Saab clubs continue to cater for ever-growing interest in this model, and the classic car fraternity is at last beginning to take notice of the attractions of the performance models.

In this book, I have given an overview of the history of the classic Saab 900, going from its design, manufacture and launch to the end of its long production run, including the turbo and convertible models. The book does not claim to be a comprehensive listing of all Saab 900 variants ever produced; I have deliberately referred principally to model designations and limited-edition cars sold in the UK, as there are simply too many subtle variations produced for individual European markets and the Americas to be included in this volume.

I hope that, whether you are a former or current owner of a Saab 900 (and there are many that have owned multiple examples of the 900 range during its long production run), or an enthusiast for the model, that you enjoy this publication.

Richard Horner
Greenwich, United Kingdom

Chapter 1
Design, Manufacture
and Launch

The Saab 900 was a compact, luxury executive car, which built upon the success of the company's previous model, the Saab 99, designed by Sixten Sason. The latter had taken the Saab brand upmarket in its ultimate guise: the luxuriously appointed and fast three-door Saab 99 EMS turbo, launched in 1977. This vehicle stunned the motoring press and the public alike with its blistering performance, good fuel economy and executive car comfort. It was the world's first mass-produced turbocharged car, and brought together Saab's considerable rally and engine development expertise with Scania's turbocharging skills.

The Saab 99 series was already becoming long in the tooth by the time the EMS turbo was unleashed, having been launched way back in 1967 as a two-door saloon with a 1709cc engine. This was originally developed by Triumph and Ricardo, but it was greatly improved by Saab engineers. A four-door saloon soon followed in 1970.

The Saab 99 EMS turbo, unveiled at the Frankfurt Motor Show in 1977 and launched in the UK in March 1978, was the car that propelled Saab into the global executive car market. With a blistering 0–60 acceleration of 8.5 seconds and a maximum speed of 120 mph, the world's first luxury mass-produced turbocharged car was a superb all-round performer that gave Saab worldwide acclaim. (Richard Horner)

Over the succeeding years, enlarged 1854cc and 1985cc B-series engines joined the range and, significantly, a three-door coupé (i.e., a hatchback, or, in the US, a wagonback) was added in 1974, followed by a five-door version in 1976.

Saab buyers quickly recognised the usefulness of the combi coupé concept, which gave a massive low-level rear-loading space and plenty of room for four passengers to travel in comfort. With the rear seat base moved forward and the seat back folded down, the cargo load increased even further to an impressive 56 cubic feet – enough to load a 6-foot grandfather clock in the back.

It came as no surprise then that, when faced with impending stricter collision safety standards from US regulators in Autumn 1978 and the urgent need to design a new model within a constrained budget, Saab adopted a 'half and half' approach to the design and engineering of the car.

Saab's chief design engineer Björn Envall took half of the design from the existing Saab 99 model, while the rest was entirely new. The new, larger car was designated the Saab 900.

The Saab 99 three-door combi coupé body from the A pillar to the rear bumper was retained, but everything ahead of the A pillar was new.

It was decided to extend the front wheelbase by 50 mm and deepen the front windscreen base by 35 mm, while alterations were made to the front floor pan, bulkhead and engine bay structures to add strength to the front of the car. The net effect was an increase in the overall length of the combi coupé by 20 mm.

A new, neater and extended clamshell bonnet with twin air vents was fitted. The entire front end of the car was redesigned too, with the headlights, grille and corner lights forming a much neater and more harmonious line beneath the bonnet edge than on the Saab 99.

Safety

Passive and active safety were key attributes of the new car. The modified front section was designed to withstand an offset 30-mph collision; this was a new US standard, one which Saab met way ahead of other European manufacturers.

In the event of an accident, the front and rear ends of the car were designed to deform within crumple zones. In a severe frontal impact, the engine was also designed to push downwards. The bonnet was also designed to deform, but not hit the windscreen. Effective C-shaped collars welded to the front wings held it in place. Immensely strong, 25-mm-thick windscreen rails welded to the bulkhead added to the structural integrity of the front end.

The flanks of the Saab 900 were protected by thick, rectangular steel reinforcing members in the doors, while the three-section collapsible steering wheel column was strengthened by a honeycomb steel cage and steel bar, designed to absorb the force of the driver being thrown against the steering wheel in a collision. The passenger shell was further protected by steel members, rugged steel sections and reinforcements.

Outside this rigid safety shell, steel-backed front and rear bumpers were filled with plastic cells, which, in the event of a low-speed parking accident, just

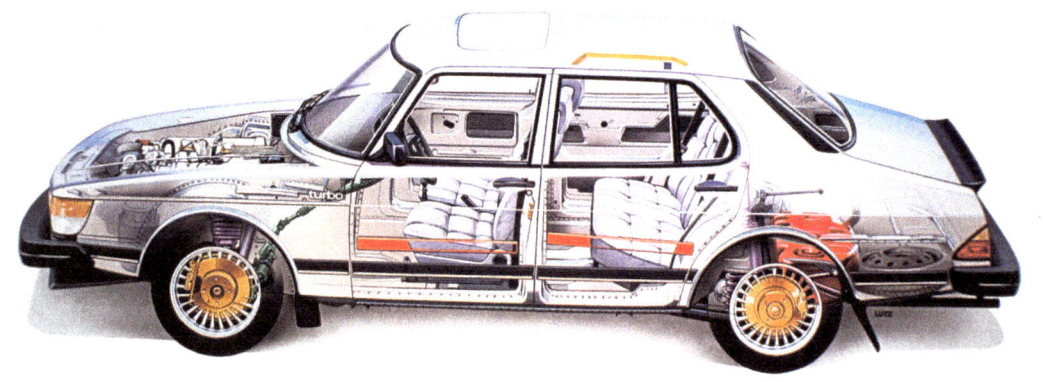

Safety was built into the new Saab 900. This cutaway drawing of the Saab 900 four-door saloon shows some of the key structural reinforcements. (Keith Long/SOC Archive)

recovered their shape. The fuel tank was suspended between the rear wheels and ahead of the boot area, the safest place possible in the event of a rear-end collision.

Inside, the driver and passenger were protected by a heavily padded steering wheel, soft knee rolls and a more rigid foam material, wrapped around the steel door inserts. The door handles were inset into a neat plastic recess in the door. Unusually, the ignition lock and key were positioned below the centre console, out of range of the knees in the event of an accident. This innovation was pioneered on the earlier Saab 99. In the rear, inertia reel and lap seatbelts were fitted as standard.

Controls were grouped around the driver in zones, so that they logically fell to hand. For example, the radio was mounted high in the dashboard, so that the view of the road was uninterrupted when inserting a cassette tape, or switching on the radio.

The rotary fan switch, temperature and air distribution controls were grouped together under the radio, with the six-position air-distribution controller used the most located nearest to the steering wheel. The least-used push switches, such as those for the emergency hazard lights and heated rear window, were located alongside the cigarette lighter, under the heating controls. The rotary switch for the headlights was located on the top-right corner of the dashboard, where it was easy to find quickly in the dark.

The zoned fascia was designed in such a way that, even if warning lights or instruments came on when the driver was concentrating on the road ahead, he would be instantly aware of them in his peripheral vision.

The easily understood, pin-sharp VDO display dials were illuminated by a cool green light when the side/headlights were switched on, and this could be dimmed if required. The substantial asymmetrical curved and moulded plastic dashboard took its cue from Saab's aircraft heritage, and echoed that of a cockpit. All controls faced towards the driver; a small plain glovebox, bearing the words 'Saab 900' in a silver band, was provided on the front passenger side.

The low, curved, wraparound windscreen not only mimicked that of an aeroplane, but it also allowed a commanding, panoramic 180-degree view of the outside world, with the angled front screen pillars so slim that they largely eliminated blind spots to driver vision at junctions. In the event of an accident, the convex curved windscreen also meant that it was unlikely that restrained front passengers would hit the windscreen.

All early Saab 900 models built between 1978 and 1979 featured a front-mounted eight-cylinder Saab B-type engine. It was canted to the left at an angle of 45 degrees. The cast-iron cylinder block was married to an aluminium alloy cylinder head with four cylinders in line, two valves per cylinder. A single camshaft was mounted in the cylinder head and operated valves in inverted bucket tappets driven by a duplex chain from the front of the forged-steel crankshaft. The clutch was at the front of the engine and the end of the flywheel faced the rear of the engine bay. The drive was taken by three Renolds chains to the four-speed gearbox, located beneath the engine.

The Saab 900 was front-wheel drive, and the steering was rack and pinion, which provided a good feel for the road. Power-assisted steering, specifically developed for the model by US manufacturer Saginaw in conjunction with Saab engineers, enabled complex manoeuvring in tight spaces to be achieved with ease (this could be hard work on the Saab 99 models!). The steering was 3.7 turns, lock to lock.

The servo-assisted braking system was very effective and reassuring for the driver, with progressive stopping action and little fade. Large ventilated 280-mm-diameter discs up front and 270-mm discs on the rear wheels provided the stopping power on diagonally split dual circuits. The handbrake operated on the front wheels only.

The front wheels were mounted in lightweight, but strong, double wishbones. The front coil springs were pivot mounted, so they were always perpendicular to the road, and any buckling tendencies were eliminated. High-quality, gas-filled shock absorbers could withstand long stretches of pounding motoring.

At the rear, a tubular dead-axle design with two forward and two rear longitudinal links (Watts linkages), located by trailing arms, and a transverse Panhard rod contributed greatly to the directional stability of the Saab 900 and its consistent, excellent road behaviour.

The weight distribution unladen was 60 per cent to the front and 40 per cent to the rear, changing to 51 per cent and 49 per cent when fully laden. It was a refined chassis design, which gave the car reassuring roadholding and immense cornering stability.

The Driving Experience

Driving the Saab 900 was a civilised and rewarding driving experience with no surprises, and, in the turbo models, huge fun. Even in the event of a high-speed front-tyre blowout, which could have unpredictable consequences in any vehicle, the Saab 900 was able to forge on, with the driver in total control. In fact, during the long production run of the Saab 900, Saab brand ambassador and rally legend Erik Carlsson used to attend promotional events and drive the car at high speed over a blade designed to puncture the front tyre to prove just this point.

Saab made much of its brand-new cabin air filter, fitted to every 900 model ahead of the bulkhead and under the bonnet. Air was channelled in through the right-hand louvre in the bonnet and passed through the filter, before entering the interior of the car. This was a first for a production car and eliminated small airborne particles and was therefore a boon to hay fever and allergy sufferers.

The car was easy to enter and exit, too. Instead of a conventional sill, the doors wrapped neatly right over the edge of the floor pan, ensuring that drivers and passengers with mobility issues found the Saab 900 a more attractive proposition than conventional cars. On the downside, the floor pedals were slightly offset to the left on right-hand drive cars, and were quite close together, which meant the driver had little space to rest his or her left foot.

Saab car seats were, in 1979, among the very best in the automotive industry. They were ergonomically designed, and extremely comfortable for long-distance and motorway driving. The early front seats fitted to the Saab 900 were nicknamed 'tombstone' seats, as they were tall and tapered slightly towards the headrest, which made it difficult for back-seat passengers to engage fully in conversation with their front-seat counterparts. Yet, whichever model you bought, the seats were supremely comfortable over long distances. Front seats featured the Klippan inertia reel seat belt. In this quirky, but safe, design, the seat belt webbing was secured in a ratcheted steel clasp instead of clip and buckle.

Investment

Series production of the Saab 900 commenced at Saab's main plant at Trollhättan near Gothenburg, Sweden, in September 1978. The plant received a substantial investment of 80 million Swedish kronor to improve production methods in readiness (mainly through deployment of robotised welders and body trucks to move body shells around the plant). It quickly became apparent, however, that this site alone would not be able to meet the rapidly growing worldwide demand for the car.

Manufacture of the Saab 900 model was, therefore, also started up at the Saab-Valmet factory in Uusikaupunki, Finland, and at a site at Arlöv near Malmö in Sweden. In 1989, a new production facility opened at Malmö, but this closed in 1990 due to the worldwide recession and a necessity for Saab to cut costs. A limited number of three-, four- and five-door Saab 900 cars were produced there.

The Uusikaupunki assembly plant became solely responsible for the production of the two-door Saab 900 saloon and the convertible on which it was derived, but it also produced three-, four- and five-door models. At Saab manufacturing plants, both group assembly and production line assembly methods were deployed during the Saab 900's fifteen-year-long run.

Launch

The Saab 900 was launched to the world at the 1978 Geneva Motor Show. The first models to be seen in the UK – a five-door GLE automatic in Aquamarine-Blue metallic and a three-door turbo in Acacia-Green metallic – appeared at the October 1978 Motor Show, held at the National Exhibition

Centre in Birmingham. Right-hand drive versions weren't actually delivered to UK Saab customers until March 1979.

The initial models launched in the UK were the 900 GL, the 900 GLS, the 900 GLE, and the 900 EMS and 900 turbo. The GL and EMS versions were only available as three-door models, while the GLS and Turbo models were available in three and five-door configurations. The GLE, marketed as a luxury five-door saloon, was only available with Borg-Warner automatic transmission.

All five-door versions included an unusual 'opera window' to allow extra light through the C pillar into the rear of the car. This feature was carried over from the 99 combi coupé but, to many Saab enthusiasts, this spoiled the look of an otherwise clean and stylish design.

The 900 GL was the base model and featured the 1985cc B-series engine carried over from the Saab 99, with a single Zenith-Stromberg 175 CDSEVX horizontal carburettor, developing 100 bhp.

The 900 GLS was similar in specification to the GL, but featured twin Zenith-Stromberg 150 CDSEVX horizontal carburettors, developing 108 bhp. It was available in both three- and five-door versions. Both GL and GLS models featured fairly plain polyester velour interiors, without rear headrests, and had steel wheels painted silver with polished steel centre caps.

The 900 GLE and EMS versions both featured Bosch K-Jetronic fuel injection and developed 118 bhp. These models had luxury, deep velour interiors and power steering as standard. Although both were very well appointed in their own right, the EMS, with its attractive 'soccer ball' wheels and identical interior to the turbo model, was marketed as a sporty alternative to its more sophisticated sister.

The 900 three- and five-door turbos carried on the success of the ground-breaking Saab 99 EMS turbo, launched to the UK press in February 1978. They featured the same B-series eight-valve engine as the 99 turbo, fitted with the oil-cooled Garrett AiResearch T3 turbocharger, developing 145 bhp, and a Saab-developed wastegate. The wastegate was fitted with a valve, which opened when the charge air pressure reached a set level and the waste gases were diverted into the exhaust system.

Apart from the key 900 design changes highlighted above, the 900 three-door turbo was virtually identical inside and outside to its 99 EMS turbo predecessor, featuring deep velour and vinyl-backed seats, with large integral headrests front and rear and cast-alloy Inca turbo-vane wheels. The five-door featured an attractive hatched-pattern velour and had multi-spoked light alloy wheels on metric rims. These were fitted with Michelin TRX tyres for an even more comfortable ride.

All models featured as standard a headlamp wash-wipe and a heated driver's seat, which turned on automatically whenever the engine was started with the external temperature below 14 degrees Celsius. The GLE and five-door turbo models also featured a heated passenger seat. Power steering was standard on all automatic and turbo versions, and optional on the GLS.

Unpainted body shells are spot-welded by robotic arms in this view of the Trollhättan Saab 900 production line in 1979. Human welders also finished the body shells prior to painting. (Saab Car Museum)

In this section of the assembly line at Trollhättan, skilled welders make additional spot welds to the body shells of three- and five-door Saab 900s not covered by the robotic welding process. (Saab Car Museum)

This October 1980 image shows a newly launched four-door Saab 900 body shell on the Finnish Uusikaupunki production line having excess weld ground off at the corner of the roof line and rear window aperture. On all models, this weld line was covered by a black plastic gutter strip. The photo also demonstrates the immense strength of the body shell. (Valmet Automotive)

Unpainted body shells were moved around the Trollhättan car plant using mechanised body trucks. Saab invested 80 million Swedish kronor in modernising the facility before Saab 900 production commenced. (Saab Car Museum)

In this 1979 view, white-painted Saab 900 body shells progress through the paint shop section at Saab's Trollhättan plant. (Saab Car Museum)

After paint-drying, doors were removed from the cars so that internal fit-out could take place on the assembly lines. They were restored to the cars at a later stage in the production process. (Saab Car Museum)

The rear suspension unit of a white Saab 900 five-door is married up to the car on the Trollhättan production line in this 1981 view. As can be seen, the suspension units were fully made up before being bolted to the body shell. (Saab Car Museum)

The dashboard was delivered to the production line as a complete assembly, whose functionality was fully tested on the bench before being fitted to the car. In this 1979 view, a white left-hand-drive, five-door Saab 900 turbo with sunroof is being fitted with the distinctive curved dashboard. The windscreen, windscreen pillar covers and foot pedals have already been fitted. (Saab Car Museum)

Left: These left-hand-drive cars, seen at the final assembly stage of the production line at Trollhättan in March 1986, are intended for the US market. US Saab 900s at this time had a different headlight arrangement from those destined for European markets, with the driving lights set into a grey plastic moulding. European cars featured integrated halogen headlights, mounted flush with the front grille. (Saab Car Museum)

Below: Doors are mounted on the painted Saab 900 body shells progressing along the Trollhättan assembly line in 1982. The doors are kept in racks either side of the line until needed. Three-door and five-door hatchbacks proceed along the line, with the four-door saloon variant also available at this time seen in the middle distance.
(Saab Car Museum)

Above: Final assembly of a 1979 Saab 900 turbo three-door with the early B-series engine at Trollhättan. At this stage, all key mechanical components and dashboard have been fitted to the car, with wheels, grille, lights, bumpers, doors, bonnet, side windows and interior to be fitted. Note the limited protection to bodywork from accidental damage such as scuffing. (Saab Car Museum)

Right: The 250,000th Saab car, produced at the Uusikaupunki car plant in Finland, was a four-door left-hand-drive Saab 900 turbo model, which was finished on 10 March 1982. Saab and Valmet Automotive entered into a partnership to produce Saab cars in 1968, and the first Saab cars produced in Finland were 96 V4 saloons and 95 V4 estates, followed by the 99 series, one of which is seen behind the milestone car. (Valmet Automotive)

A very rare publicity shot of one of the first completed Saab 900s from the Saab-Valmet plant in Uusikaupunki, Finland. Set against a typical Finnish snow backdrop, with distinctive rally-style 900 decals on the driver's door, this shot just oozes style. This 900 GLS model features the thinner protective side mouldings and twin bonnet vents found only on the 1979 model-year cars. (Valmet Automotive)

This model-launch photo shows the 1979 Saab 900 GL in Chamotte Brown. The GL base model featured a fairly basic nylon velour interior, and steel wheels painted silver with a stainless steel centre cap. This model has no sunroof and the rear windows are fixed, rather than opening. (Saab Car Museum)

The 1979 Saab GLE five door featured Bugatti 35-style stainless steel wheels, and automatic transmission was standard. This rare car, the seventeenth off the production line and intended for the US market, is now kept at the Saab Car Museum, Trollhättan, Sweden. (Saab Car Museum)

A 1980 Saab 900 turbo in black with Inca alloy wheels and revised front seats, which featured a vertically adjustable headrest. These replaced the previous 'tombstone' front seats with a headrest insert, which often popped out. Positioned correctly, the revised headrests significantly reduced the risk of serious whiplash injury in the event of an accident. (Saab Car Museum)

Chapter 2
Continuous Improvement

Saab never had huge sums of money to invest in new models, so in most of its long-lived model ranges, such as the Saab 96 and 99, continuous improvement to the line-up over the years was the name of the game. This also proved true for the Saab 900 range, which lasted in production for an impressive fifteen years.

Although the first and last Saab 900 coupés and convertibles were outwardly similar, underneath the body skin many significant improvements were made along the way. Some of these reflected marketplace changes (such as the introduction of ABS braking and catalytic converters); others were subtle but important improvements developed by Saab engineers to improve the car's characteristics. Many were industry leading, such as Saab's development of asbestos-free brake pads.

By the time the model was in its last year of production, many features earlier specified as an option had become standard, such as electric mirrors, electric sunroof, air-conditioning, heated front seats for both driver and front-seat passenger, and radio/cassette player and electric aerial. Although the body shape was becoming dated by 1993, a canny Saab 900 buyer then would have benefitted from one of the most highly specified luxury cars of the era at a great price.

For the 1980 model year (Saab model years run from October the prior year to the subsequent September: i.e., October 1979 to September 1980), which was a year after launch, the EMS and turbo models received a five-speed gearbox. This improved the overall appeal of these models against competitors in the executive sector.

All models received a revised rear-light cluster, which was larger and clearer than the previous design. The silver strip to the top of the cluster was deleted. In addition, the front seats were restyled, and received vertically adjustable headrests.

The twin-vent bonnet was also dropped, in favour of a single-vent unit situated on the right-hand side. Incoming air passed through it to reach the cabin filter. It was found that the second vent made little difference to engine cooling as originally intended. The 900 badge was removed from the bonnet edge and placed on the tailgate.

Many minor improvements were made to the 1981 model-year cars. Most significant were the revision of the front-seat runners, back-seat cushions, and backrests, and a reduction in the height of the floor tunnel, so as to create more space for rear-seat passengers. The Klippan seatbelt clasp changed to a conventional plug-in type. The spare wheel, now with a space-saver tyre, was moved from an upright position in the boot to under the load floor. A revised, larger-capacity fuel tank was also installed, increasing from 55 to 63 litres. New wing mirrors were provided, positioned at the corner of the front windows. These were manually adjustable from inside the car.

A brand-new H-series engine, developed by Saab engine expert Karl-Eric Peterssen and his team, was introduced. This gave a 10 per cent weight saving over the previous B-series engine. The idler shaft, driving the distributor, oil, fuel and water pumps, was replaced by a new, lighter distributor, driven from the camshaft. This drove the oil and fuel pumps, while the water pump was now driven by a conventional alternator belt. This enabled a simpler, lighter block to be cast and installed.

The 900 turbo model received an updated front spoiler with a grey metallic finish and rubber lip. A new four-spoke steering wheel with impact protection over the lower half became standard. New, thicker side-body mouldings became standard across all variants.

A number of changes were made to 1982 model-year cars. New, lighter, steel wheels were fitted across the sub-turbo model range. The Saab 900 turbo and EMS models now featured the five-speed gearbox as standard. Central locking became standard on most models. The 900 GL, a new base model that lacked power steering and sunroof, was introduced, while the Saab 900 GLS three door, which had been temporarily dropped, was reintroduced to the range. Automatic Performance Control (APC) was introduced to the turbo models (see Chapter Four).

The GLE and EMS models were dropped altogether in January 1982 and replaced by the 900 GLi, which featured the eight-valve Bosch K-Jetronic fuel-injection system, developing 118 bhp.

In the 1983 model-year, a significant, but largely invisible, improvement was made to the Saab 900 braking system across all models. Spearheading change across the world's motor industry, asbestos-free brake pads were introduced by Saab after five years' continuous development. This was a significant health and safety move, which benefitted all who serviced and maintained the Saab 900.

Central locking and electric windows were fitted as standard on more models.

For the 1984 model-year, the Saab 900 front grille was revised. It now had softer lines and just one fluted vane either side of the centre section. The interior now featured revised lower front seats and delayed-shut-off interior lights. A brand-new breaker-less ignition system was also introduced across the range.

However, the biggest development of all was the release of the sixteen-valve, 175-bhp, double overhead camshaft B202 engine, developed by Per Gillbrand and his team. This was was installed in the Saab 900 T16 turbo, launched in the spring of that year. This was a far more efficient and quieter unit than the previous eight-valve H-series engine, with its four valves per cylinder domed combustion chambers and centrally positioned spark plugs, augmented by the industry-leading APC system.

In 1985, further consolidation of the Saab 900 range took place. The GLS model was dropped altogether, and the GL base model became the plain Saab 900. The single Zenith-Stromberg carburettor, eight-valve, H-series engine, developing just 100 bhp, was retained, and the 900 continued to be only available in two-door saloon format.

Even when the 900 range was restyled with integrated bumpers in 1986 (see Chapter Three), the 900 base model kept its old-style bumpers and chrome window surrounds until it was dropped altogether from the range in 1988.

The 900i (formerly the 900 GLi) featured the Bosch fuel-injected eight-valve H-series engine, developing 118 bhp, and was available in two-, three-, four- and five-door configurations.

The 900 turbo model was available as the eight-valve H-series turbocharged engine, developing 155 bhp, in three-, four- or five-door variants.

Additionally, the 900 turbo 16 three-door, developing 175 bhp, was also available. This was fitted with Saab's latest sixteen-valve double overhead camshaft engine and sold in standard form, with side protective body mouldings, or in Aero form, with side skirts.

The side skirts were developed by Saab, in conjunction with IAD of Shoreham-on-Sea, UK. Not only did they add great visual appeal to the already attractive and distinctive Saab 900 body shape, but the improved aerodynamics also helped push the top speed of the model to 130 mph. The 900 turbo S, which featured lowered suspension, heavy-duty shock absorbers and anti-roll bars, gave the car an aggressive-looking stance, adding to its sporty appeal.

Other cross-model improvements included larger brake pads on the front wheels, a quieter exhaust system on the 900i, and a more powerful starter motor.

For the first time since the two companies of Saab and Scania merged, all Saab 900s carried the Saab-Scania badge on steering wheel, bonnet and tailgate (or boot) from 1985. This stylish, yet traditional, design featured a red griffin with a yellow crown on a navy blue background, encompassed within two ellipses bearing the Saab and Scania names.

For the 1986 model year, Saab fitted the base-carburettor 900 and fuel-injected 900i models with a new exhaust manifold, which preheated the air intake, enabling improved combustion and delivering improved torque. A two-door version of the eight-valve turbo was also introduced, having been developed by Saab-Valmet in Finland way back in 1981. All turbo models now featured a chrome front grille.

This 1979 Saab 900 GLS in Alabaster Yellow has been owned by one gentleman for thirty-six years and regularly attends Saab rallies across the UK. The GLS model featured twin Zenith-Stromberg carburettors and had a similar interior to the GL. (Alex Rankin)

A rear view of the same car shows the large tailgate with heated rear screen and distinctive rear Saab mud flaps. The silver top rear lamps were replaced by a new design for the 1980 model-year. (Alex Rankin)

This Acacia-Green metallic Saab 900 turbo dates from 1979 and features the B-series engine found in the previous year's Saab 99 EMS turbo. The 1979 turbo featured twin vents in the bonnet, door-mounted mirrors, 'tombstone' seats, large rear headrests and a sliding steel sunroof. The interior was similar to that found in Saab 99 EMS turbos, only with a complementary green fabric instead of red. (David Dallimore)

This cutaway drawing of a left-hand-drive version of the same Acacia-Green, three-door shows some of the key safety features of the car, including rugged steel sections in the windscreen pillars, strong steel members in the doors and specially reinforced sill beams. The 55-gallon fuel tank sits between the rear wheels, the safest position in the event of a rear-end collision. (Keith Long/SOC Archive)

This 1980 Saab 900 EMS model, finished in Cardinal-Red metallic, is a very rare survivor. It features the same plush red interior as the turbo, but has a conventional fuel-injected engine. The EMS also had distinctive 'soccer ball' alloy wheels and chrome-effect plastic wheel-arch trim. (Richard Horner)

The rear view of the 1980 Saab 900 EMS shows the plastic chrome-effect wheel-arch trim found on the early cars. The rear hatch also featured black trim above the lights and above the tailgate handle. (Richard Horner)

The four-door notchback saloon version of the Saab 900, designed by Björn Envall, was introduced in late 1980 for the 1981 model-year. This gold example is a 900 turbo version and is fitted with alloy multi-spoke wheels, tinted glass and black number plate panel. It now resides at the Saab Car Museum in Trollhättan. (Saab Car Museum)

This stunning image of the four-door production Saab 900 GLE shows off the dark-blue metallic paint and new steel wheels introduced to the Saab 900 range. (Keith Long/SOC Archive)

This immaculate Saab 900 EMS was first registered in October 1982 in Sweden, and was resold by leading Swedish Saab retailer ANA to its new UK owner in 2015. It is one of the last EMS models manufactured. It is finished in Silver metallic paint and has Saab Minilite wheels. It is now re-registered in the UK. (Stephen Miles)

A close-up of the distinctive alloy wheels shows that the rims were stamped with both Saab and Minilite names. (Stephen Miles)

A stunning low-angle shot of a 1983 Saab 900 GLE five-door car in Alabaster Yellow. The front grille had been tidied up for the 1981 model-year, losing the strange lozenge insert and giving a cleaner appearance. The body side-mouldings were thicker, yet more attractive. (Keith Long)

A rear view of the same car shows in more detail the distinctive 'opera glass' window in the rear quarter panel, found only on the five-door cars to give extra light for rear-seat passengers. This was carried over from the Saab 99 five-door combi coupé, originally launched in 1976. The design treatment was not as successful as the later four-door cars, which used the same door pressings. (Keith Long)

The 900i models featured a plastic front grille, which was painted silver-grey. This is shown to good effect on this Maroon car. Only the turbo models had a chrome-effect grille. (Keith Long)

This attractive 1985 flat-front Saab 900i is finished in Maroon with optional Super Inca alloys and attractive red pinstripes. (Keith Long)

This smart, late flat-front Black Saab 900 turbo S, with Arizona tan leather interior, was first registered in the UK in August 1986, just prior to the announcement of the restyled Saab 900 in autumn 1986 for the 1987 model-year. (David Dallimore)

The Saab 900i two-door saloon became the entry model in the UK market when the Saab 900 carburettor base model was discontinued in 1988. The two-door 900i was launched in 1984 with the H-series, eight-valve engine; when the eight-valve was dropped in 1989, the 900i two-door saloon adopted the sixteen-valve B202 engine for a short period. The two-door saloon was completely dropped by the 1991 model-year. This 900i two-door flat-front model in Malachite Green was first registered in 1987, and retains the stainless brushed-steel wheel covers specified for 900i models. (Alex Rankin)

Chapter 3
Redesign of the 900

In October 1986, for the 1987 model-year, Saab announced the restyled Saab 900 model line-up. The models produced in previous years subsequently became known as 'flat-front' Saabs, because the fundamental change to the redesigned Saab 900 was around the front grille, light and bumper assemblies.

Although generally attractive, the Saab 900 flat-front models did not appear too well integrated at the front, and this was further accentuated by the large, sturdy bumpers, which, although undoubtedly strong and heavy, did not blend in well with the surrounding bodywork. The 1986 restyling exercise under Björn Envall, Saab's chief designer, changed all these elements for the better.

First, the bumper assembly was changed so that the black rubber outer skin with silver plastic strip inserts now covered a thick foam casing, mated to a strong metal back plate.

In the event of an accident, instead of replacing the plastic cells of the earlier style of bumper, Saab dealers either replaced the foam section or the rubber bumper cover (or the complete unit). In accidents below 5 mph, the foam was self-repairing. The bumper cover was contoured around the sidelight assembly and integrated with a side moulding on the front wing, via a neat, corrugated overlap. A meshed underskirt and rubber strip appeared below the front bumper. At the rear end, the bumper cover extensions extended downwards to the bottom of the rear quarter, so that mud and muck could be more easily cleaned off.

The Saab 900 turbo models fitted with Aero body styling for the 1987 model year onwards also had the bumper extension overlap, but there was no corrugated section. The entire body kit, including front and rear bumpers, bumper extensions and aerodynamic side skirts, was painted Anthracite Grey.

Second, the front grille was completely redesigned, with a more attractive 23-degree rake. Just two types of grille were now produced across the 900 range, instead of variations for each model. These were either painted metallic silver grey (non-turbo models) or had chrome-effect silvered plastic (turbo models).

Third, the halogen headlights were made thinner and more attractive, and the sidelights redesigned to merge seamlessly into the headlight assembly and wrap around the corners. Apart from the Saab 900 base (carburettor) model, all brightwork around the windows and door handles of the Saab 900 was replaced by a matt-black finish under the restyling exercise.

Additionally for the 1987 model year, the Zenith-Stromberg carburettor on the base-model Saab 900 was replaced by a new Pierburg type so as to improve cold-start efficiency.

In 1988, further improvements were made to the mechanical side of the Saab 900. The operation of the handbrake was moved from the front wheels of the car to the rear. In addition, the larger brakes and hubs of the Saab 9000, the contemporary executive sister of the 900, were installed.

In the 1989 model-year, high-level brake lights were fitted to the rear windows of both hatchback and saloon models.

In 1990, the Saab 900 fuel-tank capacity was increased again, from 63 to 68 gallons.

In the 1991 model-year, the front seats and seat anchorage points were altered so that Saab 900-type front seats could be installed. The front seats could be moved forward to gain access to the rear by means of a catch on the side of the seat, instead of the base as before. Electrical adjustment of seats was an option on the turbo. The LVO dash instrumentation was changed to a thinner style as well.

Additionally, all models were fitted with Saab's Automatic Braking System (ABS), called ABS + 3. This was microprocessor-controlled with cross-checking electronics. There were three brake circuits – one for each front wheel and one for the rear wheels.

For the 1992 model year, there were no significant changes, apart from the introduction of catalytic converters across the entire range. The silver strip bearing the Saab 900 notation on the glove box was dropped. In the UK, the Saab 900 range was rationalised to the 900i, 900 SE (injection only) and 900 SE (light pressure turbo/LPT), and 900 turbo S models. All had air-conditioning as standard. The 900 S designation for the LPT in the UK was dropped in this final year of production.

The last classic Saab 900 coupé to be produced was a three-door Saab 900 turbo S model in Imola Red, which rolled off the Trollhättan production line on 26 March 1993 and went straight into the Saab Car Museum there. The last 900 coupé built at Uusikaupunki in Finland was despatched on 30 June 1992, but the 900 convertible was produced there for another fourteen months. (See chapter five)

This well-used 1987 Saab 900i three-door in Cirrus White demonstrates the integrated front and rear bumpers associated with that year's restyling exercise. This particular car has covered an impressive 339,500 miles from new on the original engine and gearbox, but has been modified with later Saab wheel covers. (Ann Petherick)

Rear view of the 1987 Saab 900i three-door. The retention of polished aluminium trim around the windows and plastic chrome screen inserts suggests that this car was finished before the changeover to matt black. (Ann Petherick)

An immaculate 1987 five-door 900i coupé in Midnight Blue. The 900i 1987 model year cars featured a revised front-end treatment with integrated black rubber bumpers, and a cleaner headlamp/side-indicator arrangement. Side repeaters were also fitted to the front wings behind the wheel arch. (Keith Long)

The rear view of the same car shows the simple 900i badging. Despite the five-door format, the overall length of the vehicle was the same as its three-door counterpart, taking advantage of shortened front and rear doors. The Saab 900i model had no sunroof, and featured wind-up windows and manually operated wing mirrors. By purchasing an 'S' pack, purchasers could benefit from an electric steel sunroof (as shown), electric windows and mirrors. This 'S' electrical pack must not be confused with the designation 'S' or 'turbo S', reserved for low- and high-pressure turbo models respectively. (Keith Long)

Front view of a Saab 900i five-door car in Citrin Beige metallic, first registered in 1991. The front grille on the non-turbo models was painted silver grey, which often weathered to near black over time. (Samantha Bird)

Rear view of the Saab 900i five-door in Citrin Beige metallic. A hole for an optional rear wiper arm in the hatchback glass was covered by a black plastic grommet, ready for removal and fitment. Note the revised black rubber bumpers fitted to all new Saab 900 cars after October 1986. (Samantha Bird)

By 1988, the Saab 900i eight-valve two-door saloon had become the entry-level Saab 900 after the carburettor version was finally dropped. This model was not fitted with a factory sunroof as standard, but many UK dealers offered the Saab pop-up glass sunroof as an option, as shown. These were usually fitted by local sunroof specialists near to the dealer in question. They lack the familiar lip around the front edge of the windscreen aperture found on the factory-fitted cars. (Richard Horner)

A rear view of the distinctive boot and curved rear window outline of the Saab 900i two-door saloon, designed by Björn Envall. This immaculate two-owner model features the H-series eight-valve fuel-injected engine and was first registered on 21 June 1988. (Richard Horner)

The lines of the two-door saloon, designed by Saab chief designer Björn Envall, were pleasing and, unsurprisingly, it bore very strong similarities to the four-door saloon, which was launched first, in 1980. Although first sold in the UK in 1984, evidence shows that the two-door design had been perfected by Saab-Valmet in Uusikaupunki by 1981. (Richard Horner)

Five-, three- and two-door Saab 900i versions are seen in this unusual group shot. The metallic-blue, five-door, flat-front GLi, dating from 1984, has chrome windscreen surrounds and door handles, while the other vehicles feature the restyled front end, black windscreen surrounds and door handles of the post-1986 model restyling. (Richard Horner)

A 1993 Saab 900 SE low-pressure turbo in Le Mans-Blue metallic, fitted with additional extras, including Saab/Ronal minilite wheels, whale-tail spoiler and rear window wash/wipe. Le Mans Blue was a popular Saab 900 paint choice, which, in bright sunlight, had hints of iridescent purple. (Richard Horner)

A 1992-registered five-door 900 SE in Black paint is shown at a Saab rally in the UK. The 900 SE featured grey velour seats and extras such as air-conditioning (and sunroof) in the last model-year for the Saab 900. (David Dallimore)

Chapter 4
Turbocharged Engine Models

Having produced an exceptional and much-praised turbocharged three-door coupé – the Saab 99 EMS turbo of 1977 – which both transformed Saab's fortunes and boosted its engineering credentials – it was inevitable that turbocharged engine models would form a significant part of the Saab 900 model line-up. And so it proved, as from 1979 to 1993, every model-year featured a turbo as part of the Saab offer. Indeed, in some years, one third of all Saab 900 production comprised turbo models.

The early Saab 900 turbos deployed the same eight-valve longitudinally mounted B-series engine found in the 99 turbo and produced the same output – 145 bhp.

These three- and five-door turbo models featured twin bonnet vents, thin body side mouldings and silver-edged rear light clusters. Along the bonnet sides, the 'turbo' designation was picked out in neat, lower-case, sans-serif lettering instead of the stylised design featuring a turbo vane found on the 99 EMS turbo.

The engines were coupled to the Garret AiResearch T3 turbocharger unit, which was oil cooled. The same 0–60 response time of 8.5 seconds was maintained, which gave the 900 turbo superb overtaking capabilities on twisting roads and cross country. However, this engine exhibited a degree of turbo lag, with a distinct pause of a few seconds, before road speed increased sufficiently to pin the driver back in his seat and enable preceding vehicles to be safely overtaken. Above all, however, it was a fun and reassuring drive, which was even better than the excellent Bosch fuel-injected Saab 900s, and the turbo lag was easily overcome in everyday driving.

Enter the H-Series Engine

In late 1980, for the 1981 model year, the engine was replaced by Saab's newly developed H-series eight-valve engine, coupled to a water- and oil-cooled version of the Garrett T3 AiResearch turbocharger. On the new engine, the distributor is located at the front of the cylinder head and driven by the camshaft, while the water pump is located at the rear of the engine. Additionally, a four-door saloon version of the 900 turbo was launched at the March 1980 Geneva Motor Show, featuring a rear boot and (instead of an opera window in the rear pillars) a neat, black, plastic vent along the trailing edge.

In 1982, Saab introduced Automatic Performance Control (APC) on the turbo model. APC was an important automotive industry first, and again Saab made much of it in its publicity. APC deployed a solid-state electronic knock sensor to prevent engine pinking (detonation) under load. It was designed to ensure that the engine ran at optimum efficiency at all times, by making adjustments up to twelve times a second. APC also adjusted itself to the different octane grades of petrol sold, including 95 RON and 98 RON unleaded fuels. The APC cars featured subtle APC badging on the rear hatch or boot.

In 1984, Saab launched the 900 turbo 16 model (T16) with a sixteen-valve double overhead cam engine, intercooler and turbocharger. This B202 engine had been developed by Saab engine expert Per Gillbrand during the late 1970s and early 1980s, and was produced at Saab's engine plant at Södertälje in Sweden.

The T16 had four valves per cylinder (two fuel entry and two exit ports) and hydraulic valve lifters. Overall, it was much smoother and more balanced than the eight-valve turbo, although the performance was similar, both topping out at around 130 mph.

The turbo 16 developed 175 bhp and the 0–60 mph acceleration time was an impressive 8.2 seconds. The 50–70 mph mid-range acceleration was an impressive 4.5 seconds, beating the Porsche 911 of the time.

For the 1985 Saab 900 range, Saab offered the turbo 16 S model alongside the turbo 16. The difference between the two models was that the T16S featured a roll bar and shorter, stiffer springs, which gave the car improved roadholding characteristics, as well as cruise control.

In 1986, Saab fitted an intercooler to its eight-valve turbocharged engines, raising the power output from 145 bhp to 155 bhp.

In 1989, a small number (263) of two-door 900 turbo saloons fitted with the Aero body kit and sixteen-valve turbo engine were manufactured at the Saab Valmet Uusikaupunki plant for the UK market. The stiffer two-door body shell and turbo suspension set up gave these saloons excellent roadholding capabilities and these vehicles are highly sought after by collectors today. It is not known why this model was released for one year, other than the two-door saloon was deleted entirely from the range in 1990 and there was possibly a desire to use up the body shells.

From 1991 onwards, the Garret turbocharger was replaced by a Mitsubishi TE-05, which was both smaller in size and spooled up more quickly.

Introduction of LPT Engine models

That same year, Saab introduced a low-pressure turbo (LPT) engine, which appeared in the 900 S models, and 1992 onwards 900 SE turbo models. The low-pressure turbo engine again offered a rapid performance mid-range, and also utilised the Mitsubishi TE-05 unit, but featured a different intercooler.

A tweaked version of the T16 engine appeared in the 1990-2 Carlsson and 1992-3 Ruby models, which had a red-box engine control unit (ECU), developing 185 bhp.

Only LPT 900 SE and T16S turbo models were produced and sold in the UK in the last year of Saab 900 production (1992–3), as well as the 900 Ruby limited edition (see Chapter Six).

This 900 turbo is an early 1979 example for the UK market, finished in Cardinal-Red metallic. The early 900 turbo models with the B-series engine had four-speed manual gearboxes, and featured metal-cased mirrors, mounted on the top edge of the door skin. The plush red interior retained the 'tombstone' seats and large rear headrests of the three-door Saab 99 EMS turbo that preceded it. (Alex Rankin)

Rear view of the 1979 Saab 900 turbo, with Inca alloy wheels. The early 1979–1980 Saab 900 models retained the same rear lights as the preceding Saab 99 combi coupé models, characterised by a silver strip around the top edge. The models also featured thinner side-body mouldings. (Alex Rankin)

A 1982 model-year five-door Saab 900 turbo in Aquamarine-Blue metallic with multi-spoke alloy wheels. The 1982 model featured a five-speed gearbox, revised body-side mouldings and an internally adjustable mirror, mounted at the corner of the front window. This car was first registered in October 1981 and it regularly attends Saab events across the UK. (Alex Rankin)

This five-door 1981-registered Saab 900 turbo in blue metallic paint has been modified, with body colour painted Airflow body skirts and matching painted mirrors and Saab Ronal alloys. It also features the Saab bonnet-edge protector. (David Dallimore)

This Black Saab 900 eight-valve turbo three-door with Saab's APC system was first registered in 1983, and has covered 378,000 miles in the hands of just two owners – the last for an incredible twenty-eight years. (Ian Howel)

This Saab 900 turbo in Carmine-Red metallic is a flat-front version dating from 1980, and features a number of Saab 900 extras: the swage-line rubber protective strip, Saab bonnet-edge protector and vent covers. The Inca alloy wheels were normally painted silver; these have been customised and are black. (Richard Horner)

This superb Silver Saab 900 turbo 16, first registered in November 1984, has had the same owner since August 1987, and has been maintained throughout by one Saab master technician. It is fitted with velour seating, with matching Colorado-Red dashboard and interior plastics. It has covered just 54,000 miles from new, and remains in original as-new condition except for the side skirts, which were subsequently painted to match the body colour. (Robert William James Murray)

This 1985 Saab 900 turbo 16 was left abandoned in a garage until the current owner rescued it, stripped it, restored it, repainted it and put it back together again to the highest concours standards. It is now a regular winner on the Saab show circuit, and deservedly so. (*Practical Classics*/Jason Critchell)

The immaculate engine bay of a Silver 1984 Saab 900 sixteen-valve turbo. Remarkably, this is in unrestored, as-new condition, and shows the real ease of access to the engine for servicing. On the top left is the intercooler for the turbocharger, and on the right is the slanted B202 sixteen-valve engine, introduced that year. It was developed by Saab engine expert Per Gillbrand and his team. (Robert Wiliam James Murray)

A beautifully presented Saab 900 turbo 16 interior. The deep-velour heated front seats and plush carpets added to the luxurious ambience of this top-of-the-range model. Early sixteen-valve turbos could be specified with Colorado-Red leather seats and matching dashboard, although later models were finished with dark- and light-grey dashboards. (Robert William James Murray)

This superb image captures the beauty of the 1984 Saab 900 turbo sixteen-valve well. The Silver paintwork and Colorado-Red leather interior are an acquired taste today, but this combination was not at all rare for Saab turbo customers in the 1980s.
(*Practical Classics*/Jason Critchell)

The Colorado-Red interior of this 1984 Saab 900 turbo includes matching dashboard, carpets, leather seats and gear-lever gaitor. Leather seats were an optional extra on this model. The matching leather steering wheel and supplementary gauges were also options.
(*Practical Classics*/Jason Critchell)

A Saab 900 three-door turbo, with standard body mouldings and 15-inch alloy wheels, is shown glinting in the sun in Cherry Red. (David Dallimore)

A stunning Saab 900 turbo S on show at a Saab club event. The car is finished in Le Mans-Blue metallic and features the later Saab leather seats with suede inserts. It is fitted with the Saab Aero body kit, although the deep-dish alloys are not original to the Saab 900. (David Dallimore)

This beautifully restored 1988 Saab 900 turbo 16S is one of 263 sold in the UK in 1988/9 in two-door format, with a stiffer body shell compared to the hatch version. A regular star on the UK rally circuit, it is finished in Odoardo metallic grey paint. (David Dallimore)

This low-down shot of a similar 1990 Saab 900 turbo S sixteen-valve three-door car in Odoardo Grey neatly demonstrates the streamlined front achieved by the body styling, and the mesh grille and rubber lip under the front bumper. (David Dallimore)

A Saab 900 turbo three-door coupé and 900i two-door saloon are seen together at a Saab Owners Club National Rally in the UK. Both are finished in the Odoardo-Grey metallic paint scheme, which was one of Saab's most popular and enduring paint finishes throughout the 1980s. The Odoardo name was a tribute to Odoardo Pagani, Saab's importer for Turin, Italy. (Richard Horner)

The Saab 900 turbo 16, with its Anthracite-Grey body skirts designed by IAM of Shoreham-on-Sea in conjunction with Saab, always looked imposing in metallic Silver paint finish. Two such examples are shown at a Saab Owners Club rally in the UK. (Richard Horner)

This Saab 900 turbo 16 S in Black features the complementary Buffalo-leather interior, which was available as a popular option on this model. Apart from the 185-bhp Ruby, which had a higher output engine, the 900 turbo S had it all: electric sunroof and mirrors, air-conditioning, heated front seats, adjustable headlamps, wash-wipe and cruise control. Combined with astonishing performance and great roadholding, the young executive could not want for more. (Richard Horner)

This much-loved 1993 Saab 900 turbo S in Black, with asymmetrical Super Aero alloys, features standard grey cloth upholstery and a Saab bonnet-edge protector. It has had four owners since new, and is also upgraded by an Abbot T8 charge cooler conversion. (Richard Horner)

Chapter 5
The Saab 900 Convertible

If it hadn't been for the foresight and determination of one man, it is doubtful if the Saab 900 convertible would have been born at all. That man was Robert J. Sinclair, president of Saab-Scania America from 1979 to 1991.

Saab was planning to launch the economy 900 two-door saloon model into the American market in the early 1980s, but Sinclair understood that what American buyers actually wanted from Saab was a more upmarket model and decided against chasing the economy sector.

It was Sinclair who first suggested to Saab that they produce a high-specification four-seater turbocharged convertible (termed a cabriolet in many markets) to broaden the 900 range and add value to the Saab marque in America. Other manufacturers, worried about ever-tightening safety legislation, had ceased selling convertibles in the US, so Saab would have a market advantage if a 900 convertible could be manufactured.

Producing such a vehicle is no easy task, as it involves considerable strengthening of the floorplans and stiffening the bodyshell to retain structural rigidity, and then engineering the folding convertible roof so that it not only works easily, but also looks attractive.

Fortunately, Sinclair had a strong contact list at the American Sunroof Company of Southgate, Michigan, and they were approached by Saab to develop a prototype vehicle for consideration, with an initial development capital of $30,000 USD.

In fact, two convertible prototypes were developed: one a targa top based on the three-door coupé body style produced by the Saab design department in Trollhättan; the other fully open-top and based on the two-door saloon, produced at the Saab-Valmet plant at Uusikaupunki in Finland. Both were given a white mother-of-pearl finish, with a white folding roof.

It was decided that the Finnish example, based on the two-door bodyshell, was the most attractive from all angles.

The development work on the convertible saw not only underbody strengthening, but a complete redesign of the A pillars so that, if the car flipped onto its roof, the occupants would be properly protected. Thus, the thickness of the pillars was increased dramatically, and the rake adjusted, so that the top rail was 100 mm further back than the standard 900 coupé. The entire windscreen was redesigned to add top and side strength, which meant that the curvature and wraparound are different to the saloon version. The convertible-specific windscreen was also bonded to the frame to add strength.

The sills were also strengthened by 70-mm-high steel reinforcements, using 2.5-mm sheet steel, so that, upon entering the car, there was a distinct climb over the sill edge. Additionally, two transverse steel members, positioned beneath the back seats and the rear-seat backrest, were provided and the B pillars were beefed up by reinforced, upright steel members.

The electrically operated hood could not be activated unless the vehicle was completely stationary, but could be raised in just 30 seconds.

More than 300 components differed between the Saab 900 convertible and the two-door saloon upon which it is derived, including the wing mirror mounts, which are unique to the convertible.

Stylistically, the car featured an attractive rising waistline, with thick plastic trim forming a very attractive curved lip, just above the boot level. The triple-layered hood was raised and lowered by depressing a switch on the centre console. Hidden motors behind the seats pushed the roof upwards or downwards. The hood was located manually by latches at the corners of the top windscreen rail. An attractive plastic tonneau cover could be purchased to hide the hood mechanism when the roof was down. The rear window was genuine glass with heated rear elements, giving a quality finish not found on lesser manufacturer's models that had pop-out acrylic or plastic rear screens.

The Finnish prototype was first displayed at the 1983 Frankfurt Motor Show to gauge public reaction. Fortunately for Saab, the response from dealers and potential customers alike was both enthusiastic and unequivocal – the company must produce a convertible!

Into Production
In April 1984, the Saab board gave the go-ahead to start manufacturing the 900 convertible. Production cars differed from the prototype, in that there was more room for the rear occupants, making it a true four-seater car.

Manufacture was entrusted to the Saab-Valmet Uusikaupunki plant, as it had considerable experience in producing one-offs and limited-production-run specialist cars. The Saab 900 convertible was, to all intents and purposes, a hand-built car, with around twelve cars being produced every week at Uusikaupunki. This increased to twenty cars a week in the late 1980s. The Finnish assembly workers built up considerable skill and expertise in assembling the components of the ASC-supplied hood off the car, and then fitting and testing it.

The first 400 Saab convertibles were all reserved for the US market. They were delivered to customers in mid-1986. All models were badged '900 turbo', used the 175-bhp B202 T16 engine and featured the standard bumpers and body mouldings of the turbo saloon model. These 400 flat-front cars are rarities today as, in autumn 1986 (for the 1987 model year), the 900 turbo convertible body was revised to incorporate the facelift design (see Chapter Three), giving it a sleeker and more attractive appearance.

In 1990, Saab announced the addition of a normally aspirated model to the convertible range, utilising the 128-bhp sixteen-valve fuel-injected B202 engine, and these were badged '900i'. The 900i featured deep-plush-velour upholstery as standard, with deep storage pockets in the back of the front seats, although leather upholstery was also offered as an option.

In 1991, the 145-bhp, low-pressure, turbo, sixteen-valve B202 engine joined the convertible range and these models were badged '900 S'. Again, the standard interior finish was deep plush velour upholstery for this model, although leather could also be specified.

Also that year, the Aero body kit was made available on the convertible range, appearing as 900 S 145-bhp, low-pressure turbo-engined cars or 175-bhp, 900 turbo S-engined cars. The 900 turbo S featured anti-roll bars, sturdier shock absorbers and cruise control.

The last classic 900 convertible, an Imola-Red 900 turbo S, rolled off the Uusikaupunki production line on 14 September 1993; some 48,895 convertibles were produced in total.

As a footnote, the Lynx Engineering company in the UK hand-built two targa-type convertibles in early 1984 for customers. One was finished in Iridium Blue, the other in Cherry Red. Today only the latter, powered by an eight-valve H-series engine, survives on the road.

The two cars used the Saab 900i two-door bodyshell. They featured a strong yet attractive I-bar across the B pillars, similar to that found on the Porsche targa, with two detachable targa panels over the front seats and a small folding hood over the rear seats. The cost of the custom conversion from a two-door saloon was a then-considerable £3,000 above the Saab list price and, as soon as Saab announced that they intended to go into full production with the 900 turbo convertible, Lynx ceased marketing their version.

The prototype unpainted Saab 900 turbo convertible body shell is shown in a corner of the Uusikaupunki assembly plant at the development stage. The additional welded supports to the sills and massively reinforced windscreen surround are clearly visible. (Valmet Automotive)

Saab-Valmet design and development engineers pore over the blueprints of the first Saab 900 turbo convertible. (Valmet Automotive)

One of the first batch of Silver 900 turbo convertibles destined for the US is shown at the final assembly stage at Uusikaupunki. (Valmet Automotive)

A view of a Cirrus-White partially completed Saab 900 turbo convertible on the assembly lines in Finland. (Valmet Automotive)

A general view of the assembly lines at Uusikaupunki, Finland. Saab-Valmet employees are shown working on a Saab 900 convertible, and four-door saloon versions of the Saab 900. Note the piled-up brake lines awaiting installation. (Valmet Automotive)

An orange-jacketed quality-control inspector takes a close interest in the finish of a Cirrus-White Saab 900 convertible on the assembly line in Uusikaupunki. Note that the headlights and wheel-arch trim have already been fitted, before the rest of the bodywork. (Valmet Automotive)

An interesting production-line photo taken at Uusikaupunki, Finland, in March 1986, of four Silver Saab 900 turbo convertibles destined for the US marketplace. All are nearly ready for final inspection, except for the car in the centre of the line-up, which awaits fitment of its folding hood. Protective cover sheets have been placed over the boot and side panels in anticipation of fitment. (Valmet Automotive)

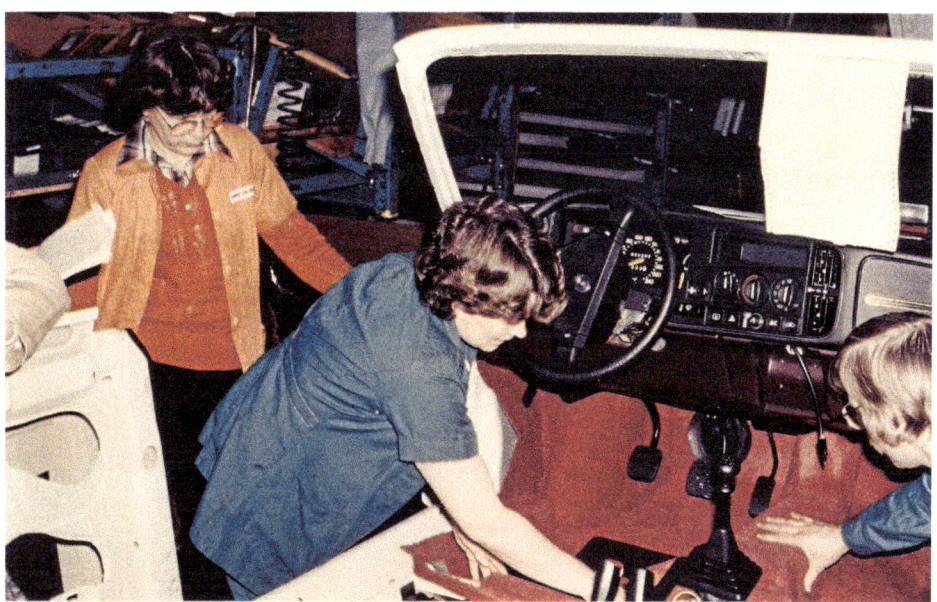

Female production-line workers at the Finnish Saab-Valmet plant in Uusikaupunki fit a dark-red carpet to a Cirrus-White Saab 900 convertible, overseen by a quality-control inspector. The Colorado-Red interior of the Saab 900 T16 turbo has been tempered on this white convertible by the fitment of a dark-grey dashboard. The lower knee roll retains the Colorado-Red shade. (Valmet Automotive)

The pre-production Saab 900 convertible was finished in mother-of-pearl white, with Colorado-Red leather interior. It was unveiled at the 1983 Geneva Motor Show to great acclaim and series production began in 1986, initially for the US market. The interior of the production models accommodated four seated adults comfortably. The prototype survives today in the Saab Car Museum, Trollhättan, Sweden. (Saab Car Museum)

All Saab 900 convertibles produced at Uusikaupunki, Finland, from 1986 to 1989 were 175-bhp turbo models, such as this flat-front, Cherry-Red example. From 1990, normally aspirated 900i and light-pressure turbo 900 S models, developing 128 bhp and 145 bhp respectively, were added to the convertible range. (Saab Car Museum)

A Cherry-Red Saab 900 turbo convertible, fitted with Anthracite-Grey body kit and asymmetric alloy wheels, looks resplendent at a Saab rally in the UK. (Alex Rankin)

The 900 S convertible featured a 145-bhp, light-pressure turbo engine. This Le Mans-Blue metallic example, dating from 1992, features the standard body mouldings and bumpers, although the model was also available with Aero body kit. (Richard Horner)

This 900 turbo 16 convertible shows the integrated look of the Odoardo-Grey metallic paintwork and Anthracite-Grey body skirts with the original silver Aero alloys. (David Dallimore)

This 1988-registered Saab 900 turbo two-litre convertible in Black features cream leather upholstery. (Cliff Mitchell)

This 900i Monte Carlo-Yellow convertible is from the 1993 model year, and features the later-style steel alloy wheels. It is one of just 892 worldwide finished in this colour. (Saab Car Museum)

Finnish inspectors examine the very last Saab 900 convertible (48,895), which rolled off the production line at Uusikaupunki on 14 September 1993. A left-hand-drive example with a beige roof, it was finished in Imola Red. Note the protective cover applied to the convertible hood before shipping. Cars were also sprayed with an external protective wax before export to Saab dealers worldwide. (Valmet Automotive)

First and last. The last classic Saab 900 turbo convertible in Imola Red and Sierra leather is shown alongside a metallic-blue, 'new generation' Saab 900 convertible, which was also produced by Saab-Valmet in Finland from 1994 until 2002. The new model was launched after General Motors took the majority share in Saab in 1991 and used many GM components to save costs. (Valmet Automotive)

The now-unique Saab 900i convertible customised by Lynx Engineering in 1984 has been lovingly been cared for by just two owners over thirty-two years. It is finished in Cherry Red and the interior is beige velour. It features two detachable targa panels over the front seats and a neat folding roof over the rear seats, divided by a sturdy hooped bar across the B pillars. (Alex Rankin)

A view of the front of the Saab 900i Lynx convertible. It was first registered in March 1984, literally just before Saab made the decision to go into production with its own convertible. The front bonnet, wings and windscreen are all standard 900i fitments. (Alan Maclean)

Detailed view of the folding rear roof on the Saab 900i Lynx convertible. It is a neat arrangement from a bespoke car maker, who managed without the resources of Saab and the American Sunroof Company to produce an alternative solution. (Alan Maclean)

A close-up of the targa-top roof arrangement on the Saab 900i Lynx convertible, showing the targa panels removed. Note the strengthening hoop, which goes from B pillar to B pillar. (Alan Maclean)

Chapter 6
The Impact of the Saab 900

Although Saab almost seemed reluctant to push the new Saab 900 initially (it was marketed as the 'New, longer Saab' in 1979, hardly an inspiring advertising tagline for a new executive car), it was very well received by customers, the press and Saab dealers worldwide.

It was well engineered, comfortable, safe, reliable and easier to maintain than the Saab 99 (even on the turbocharged cars, engine and ancillaries were relatively easy to access in the extended engine bay – unlike the preceding Saab 99 EMS turbo, with its crammed-in pipework and electrical connections).

It is easy to forget that, in the late 1970s, electrical and mechanical reliability could not be taken for granted in the automotive world. Some marques had such a woeful reputation for reliability that they regularly became the butt of comedians' jokes. Saab defied this trend by testing all its new models extensively in the harshest of conditions before launch, from the tundra of northern Sweden to the deserts of America. Saab only released the new Saab 900 when it was satisfied it was ready for the marketplace. It is often argued that Saab cars are over-engineered, but it was the Saab 900's style, reliability and quality that sold the car to a whole generation of customers.

The hardened hacks of the motoring press were impressed by the versatility, engineering and performance of the Saab 900, especially the turbo versions. Their main gripes with the car were with the gearbox (not slick and certainly not suitable for racing starts!), fuel economy and the price relative to other, smoother six-cylinder cars in the executive sector. Dealers weren't exactly numerous either, and spares imported from Sweden could be expensive. Some of the early 1979 model year cars also had paintwork/corrosion issues, which were subsequently resolved by improved production-line processes.

Loyal Saab customers recognised that the Saab 900 was an altogether different beast to the Saab 99, one which was significantly improved. Recognised for being individual, artistic and discerning, they appreciated that it was a good-quality executive car, and that to own one meant that you didn't follow the herd. Saab themselves picked up on this, using Björn Borg, Ian Botham and José Carreras to promote the model, and lending cars to sportsmen and women in the equestrian, yachting and golfing arenas. It was reputedly on the shortlist as the next James Bond car, before losing out to Lotus. Better advertising throughout the mid- to late-1980s, including the brilliant 'Saab: nothing on earth comes close' tagline, drove up its appeal and sales.

Production to meet the massive global customer demand for Saab 900 increased year-on-year at Saab plants until the mid-1980s, halfway through its production run. Even then, the launch of new models that appealed to more affluent customers, such as the legendary 900 turbo T16S Aero coupé and 900 turbo convertible, kept interest in the Saab 900 alive.

It is fair to say that there was a Saab 900 for everyone, from the antiques dealer to young executive to top investment banker. The model had so many permutations that it is unlikely that two cars were ever identical. For instance, depending on body colour, a Saab 900 turbo could have a red, grey, blue or tan interior and come with two, three, four or five doors – and that was before specifying optional equipment!

By the time the Saab 900 ceased production in 1993, it had already become an automotive icon. Saab themselves called it a 'classic' in their later brochures and, today, the cult car stands tall among the automotive giants. Surviving classic 900s are much loved and much in demand. Many owners are reluctant to part with them, with some clocking up to 500,000 miles or more in well-maintained hands. Catch one if you can!

This 1983 Cirrus-White 900i four door has been in the same family since new, and it has now covered a colossal 500,000 miles. The owner receives a high-mileage award at the annual Swedish Day enthusiasts' event held in the UK. (Alastair Lawson)

Chapter 7
Saab 900 Special Editions

Over the years, a number of special-edition Saab 900s were produced for local markets across Europe and the USA, for a variety of reasons. For example, it is widely thought that the UK Anniversary model of 1989 was introduced to use up the remaining stocks of eight-valve, H-series turbo engines before they were dropped altogether in 1990. However, except possibly for the 1991–1992 XS models, most special editions offered a greatly enhanced specification including, in many cases, leather seats or body kits, for a small additional purchase price.

All Saab cars imported to the UK entered via the Port of Immingham, Humberside, and were prepared at the Saab Import Centre at nearby Stallingborough before transfer to dealerships across the country.

It is known that certain Saab 900 special editions, such as the 1990 Saab 900 SE and 1993 Ruby, were factory prepared and sent out finished from Stallingborough.

However, there is anecdotal evidence that certain special editions, such as the 1983/4 Saab 900 SE/Lux turbo and 1989/1990 Saab 900 Anniversary, were dealer prepared before handover. Specific extras, for example the Anniversary whale-tail spoiler, were shipped in the boot of the cars to be dealer fitted before customer handover.

There is a surprising number of high-specification special editions that have survived into the 21st century as collectors' cars, such as the 1990 Saab 900 SE and 900 Ruby. However, the older specials, such as the 1981 Saab 900 GLE Gold and 1983/4 900 SE/Lux turbos are almost certainly down to single figures.

This chapter identifies the known UK variants.

Saab 900 Gold (1981)
The Saab 900 Gold special edition was a four-door Saab 900 GLE in Aquamarine-Blue metallic supplied to the UK market. It had thin, gold pinstripes along the flanks of the car and gold Minilite wheels, and featured a light-blue plush-velour interior. It is believed that just one such car survives in the UK.

This 1981 Saab 900 GLE, finished in Aquamarine-Blue metallic paint, and first registered in the UK in August that year, is the only known Gold special edition still on the road. It has been regularly maintained and lovingly looked-after by its long-term owner from new. (Albert Lain)

This view of the rear of the Saab 900 GLE Gold four-door edition shows an attractive contemporary aftermarket luggage rack mounted on top of the boot lid. Some early Saab 900 convertibles were also fitted with these, the boot panel being identical. (Albert Lain)

The 1981 900 GLE Gold special edition featured gold-painted Saab Minilite wheels and had broad gold pinstripes along the length of the swage line. This car has lost its pinstripes after undergoing bodywork restoration, but still looks striking with its gold wheels. (Albert Lain)

The engine bay of the 1981 Saab 900 GLE Gold special edition features the then-new H-series eight-valve single overhead cam fuel-injected engine, developing 118 bhp. The early type of oil filler on top of the aluminium cylinder head cover can also clearly be seen. (Albert Lain)

Saab 900 Special Equipment/Lux (1983–1984)

The 900 SE (Special Equipment)/Lux model was a special option for the 1983 and 1984 model years. It featured a 145-bhp, eight-valve turbo engine with APC control as standard. The package included a very attractive two-tone blue-over-silver paint finish, with the blue starting above the swage line and including bonnet, roof and hatch, with the silver below. The SE was available in three- and four-door body styles in the UK (five-door versions were available in some European markets), complete with attractive Bridge of Weir butterscotch-leather seating, electric windows and sunroof, and front chin and rear spoilers. A new-style steel wheel with oblong cut-outs along the outer edge of the wheel face was also included. It is believed that around 100 were sold in the UK.

The Saab 900 SE (or Lux) eight-valve turbo special edition was only available in the UK as a three- or four-door car. It is thought that a handful of around 100 sold by Saab dealers in the UK survives. Here is an identical French-registered left-hand drive three-door coupé, showing the same stylish blue-over-silver metallic two-tone paint finish and luxurious Bridge of Weir leather interior. (David Dallimore)

Saab 900 Tjugofem (1984–1985)

Launched in 1984 to celebrate the twenty-fifth anniversary of Saab in Great Britain, the Tjugofem was fitted with the 118-bhp, eight-valve, H-series fuel-injected engine with Bosch K-Jetronic fuel injection.

It adopted the newly launched, two-door bodyshell of the 900i saloon and was finished in metallic silver paint, with block-pattern cloth interior, matt-black window surrounds, colour-keyed grille, front spoiler and mirrors, grey and blue pinstripes with the word 'Tjugofem' in red, and a red rear reflector panel. The boot featured a rubber spoiler, as found on turbo models. Interior enhancements included an electric sunroof and a wooden gear-knob incorporating an engraved sterling silver insert, stating which car it was in the limited run of 300.

The 1984 Tjugofem model was introduced to commemorate twenty-five years of Saab in Great Britain. The two-door, H-series, eight-valve, fuel-injected car featured silver paintwork and painted silver wing mirrors, distinctive pinstripes and logos along the swage line, and front and rear (boot) spoilers, along with an inscribed silver gear knob, stating its limited-edition number. (Keith Long)

Close-up of the Tjugofem logo, showing the grey and blue and red logo pinstripes against the metallic silver paint, found on all Tjugofem special editions. (Alex Rankin)

Saab 900 CD (or Finlandia)

The 900 CD was an extended 900 turbo four-door saloon model, designed for corporate executives. It was first shown in the UK at the 1982 Birmingham Motor Show, marketed as the director's car. It was produced at the Saab plant at Arlöv near Malmö, Sweden, but principally at Uusikaupunki in Finland; hence the Finlandia connotation. The wheelbase was stretched by 200 mm to give additional legroom in the rear, and the front and rear doors were lengthened by 100 mm. The specification was largely as per the standard four-door turbo, including sunroof, but also included features such as rear reading lamps, foot cushions and adjustable rear window blinds. Very few were produced in right hand drive, so this vehicle is a particular rarity in the UK.

A rare Saab 900 CD (Finlandia), first produced in 1983. Most were manufactured at Saab-Valmet's plant in Finland, hence the Finlandia name. This director's car was expensive to produce, and purchase. This attractive left-hand-drive example has silver paintwork, and is shown outside the Uusikaupunki plant. (Valmet Automotive)

A rare right-hand-drive 900 CD with private registration is shown at a UK Saab Owners Club rally. Note the lengthened front and rear doorskins, which were extended by 100 mm. (Keith Long)

Saab 900 Jubilee (1987–1988)

The Jubilee was launched to commemorate the fiftieth anniversary of the formation of Saab, with around 200 being produced. It was based on the 900i eight-valve, three-door coupé body, and was finished in Odoardo-metallic-grey paint with buffalo-leather seats. Externally, the car featured silver and red coach-lines and a wreath logo incorporating the numeral '50' on the rear quarter panels. The Jubilee also had a chrome grille and Super Inca alloy wheels. The 900i logo on the rear tailgate was underscored by a silver Jubilee badge and a large whale-tail spoiler was fitted.

Front view of the Saab 900i Jubilee. The buffalo-leather upholstery fitted to this model can clearly be seen. It complements the Odoardo-Grey paint finish perfectly. (Alex Rankin)

The Saab 900i Jubilee was a limited-edition model produced in the UK in 1987 for the fiftieth anniversary of the formation of Saab car. All were finished in Odoardo-Grey metallic, with special pinstripes along the flanks as shown here. This is a late-registered 1988 model. (Alex Rankin)

The Super Inca alloy wheels, another extra added to the Saab 900i Jubilee, set off the three-door body shape to good effect. (Alex Rankin)

Saab 900 SE (1990)

The 900SE was a five-door 900 with the B202 series, sixteen-valve, fuel-injected engine. All had distinctive cross-spoked alloy wheels, not previously seen on the 900 series. They were fitted with a high-quality leather interior, walnut veneer fascia and chrome front grille, and were available in manual or automatic formats. A total of 300 were produced. The vast majority were finished in iridium blue metallic with mid-blue coach lines, although it is known that some customers took delivery of the model in Le Mans-Blue metallic and citrin silver.

Another identifying feature of the 900 SE is the chrome front grille. The Iridium-Blue paint finish suited the lines of the five-door Saab 900 very well. (John Daniel)

The 900 SE limited-edition model, introduced in 1990, was produced as a five-door hatchback only, available with manual or automatic transmission. Its profile from the side was distinctive, with blue pinstripes and a new design of Saab cross-spoke aluminium wheels. (John Daniel)

A rear view of the Saab 900 SE, showing the contrast between the black-painted lower tailgate panel and rear light clusters, as well as the integrated rear bumper. (John Daniel)

The beautifully finished interior of the Saab 900 SE featured a walnut dashboard overlay. All the controls in the Saab 900 were neatly and logically laid out in zones. This car features the Borg-Warner automatic gearbox with two-pedal control. (John Daniel)

The rear hatch on this Saab 900 SE features a wiper arm and wash wipe, which was standard on this limited-edition model. It was normally an optional extra on three- and five-door 900s, and usually fitted by individual Saab dealers. (John Daniel)

Saab 900 Anniversary (1989–1990)

The Anniversary was based on the three-door coupé with standard body mouldings. It was produced to mark the tenth anniversary of Saab turbocharging, and was finished in black and powered by the 155-bhp, H-series, eight-valve turbo engine. The tailgate was enhanced by Saab's large 'whale tail' in painted GRP and rubber, and the side vents were finished with unpainted grey plastic snow covers. This striking car had three parallel silver pinstripes along the entire length of both sides, incorporating the 'turbo' legend on the bonnet section. It ran on silver metallic Ronal alloys bearing Saab centre caps, and also included a rear reflective décor panel across the entire width of the bottom section of the tailgate.

It is believed every UK Saab dealer was provided with at least one example and the total production run was around 150.

The Saab 900 Anniversary eight-valve turbo runout model had Saab/Ronal wheels and silver pinstripes down each side of the car, with the word 'turbo' proudly proclaimed within on the bonnet section. (Nic Cooper)

At the rear of the car, the Saab reflective décor panel can be seen between the rear-light clusters, along with the large whale-tail spoiler. (Nic Cooper)

Saab 900 Carlsson (1990–1992)

Named after rally legend Erik Carlsson who, after retiring, became Saab's brand ambassador, this model was launched as a special in 1990. The Carlsson series was only available in Black, Cirrus White or Talladega Red, and included a unique body kit, including extended painted front- and rear-bumper mouldings not previously seen on 900s. The front bumper included two low-level Hella spotlights. The model featured a whale-tail rear spoiler, wide wheel-arch mouldings and a distinctive yet subtle Carlsson signature badge in black on the rear hatch. Unusually, the Saab-Scania griffin logo was separated from the Saab name badge, being mounted in the centre of the rear hatch.

The Carlsson received bold and stylish side decals in black or red, depending on body colour. These swept along the body sides and bonnet edge. They were complemented by fine line decals on the lower front, rear and side panels of the body kit. The exhaust pipe was split into two chrome pipes. The leather interior featured a stylish, bespoke, red-banded leather Carlsson steering wheel and, from 1991, suede seat inserts. Approximately 200 were supplied each year from 1990 to 1992, making 600 in total.

A Talladega-red Saab 900 Carlsson, showing the unique Carlsson decals in black along the body sides, and twin Hella headlights inserted into the specially developed front bumper. All 900 Carlssons were fitted with a 185-bhp, 'red top' engine control unit. Although Talladega Red was undoubtedly a popular colour when new, like most solid reds it had a tendency to fade to pink over time and it is a difficult colour to restore. (Alex Rankin)

This Black Saab 900 Carlsson features red decals along the body sides and light-grey ones around the skirts. This particular car has more than 278,000 miles under its belt and is a regular on the UK show circuit. Its superb condition is a credit to its current owner. (Nic Cooper)

The tailgate of the Saab 900 Carlsson saw the Saab badge separated from the griffin logo for the first and only time, and placed in the centre, above the latch handle. The Carlsson badge featured an italic signature and was positioned on the far right-hand side. (Richard Horner)

Above: This dramatic shot of a Black Saab 900 Carlsson clearly demonstrates the Hella front fog lights, mounted towards the bottom of the large front spoiler. (Nic Cooper)

Left: A view of the attractive Buffalo-Grey leather interior of a Saab 900 Carlsson. The Carlsson had a distinctive leather sports steering wheel with red and black bands. (Nic Cooper)

The massive whale-tail spoiler is shown to great effect in this rear-quarter view of the Saab 900 Carlsson. This example also features an optional reflective rear décor panel between the rear-light clusters. (Nic Cooper)

Close-up of the Carlsson insignia and pinstripes on the rear-quarter panel of a black car. They were both bold and stylish. The pinstripes on Talladega-red and Cirrus-white Carlssons were black. (Nic Cooper)

Saab 900 Monte Carlo Convertible (1991)

Around 300 Saab 900 turbo S convertibles were produced in 1991 with a striking and attractive Monte Carlo-Yellow paint finish. These convertibles had Buffalo-leather upholstery, and all featured a gear knob with the edition number etched into a silver insert.

The distinctive Monte Carlo-Yellow shade continued to be available on convertibles only into the 1992 and 1993 model years, but it could be specified across the 900i, 900 S and 900 turbo S model ranges. Although these cars did not feature limited-edition serial numbers, in total no more than 892 Monte Carlo-Yellow convertibles across all three model choices were produced worldwide, making it a very scarce Saab 900.

A limited-edition 1991 Saab 900 turbo S convertible in Monte Carlo-Yellow with Anthracite-Grey skirts, numbered 152 of 300, is shown at a Saab event in the UK. (Alex Rankin)

This Saab turbo S convertible, first registered in 1993, shows off the Monte Carlo-Yellow paint finish well, after a good polish at a Saab rally. The optional Saab bridge spoiler is also shown to great effect, also finished in gleaming yellow. (Richard Horner)

Saab 900 XS (1991–1992)

The Saab 900 XS was introduced in 1991 in the UK, in both three-door and five-door versions, as a feature-packed car within the sub two-litre tax bracket –it was designed to attract executive car buyers. The three-door featured a manual sliding sunroof and the five-door an electric sliding sunroof. Both versions had distinctive parallel-pattern velour seats, electric windows and mirrors, and headlight elevation control and a high-level rear brake light. Solid and metallic colours from the 1991–1992 colour range were standard on the 900 XS, and automatic transmission and leather seats were factory-fitted optional extras.

This well-travelled UK-registered car, shown on tour in Norway accompanied by an earlier Saab 96 saloon, is a five-door 1991 Saab 900 XS in Cirrus White. (Iain Hodcroft)

The five-door Saab 900 XS featured an electric sunroof instead of the manual version found on the three-door. As metallic paint was a standard no-cost option on the Saab 900 XS, it was unusual for this model to be ordered as a solid colour. (Iain Hodcroft)

83

The Saab 900 XS was available in the UK in the 1991/2 model-year. The feature-rich specification included turbo-style alloy wheels, Sony 7071 radio cassette, parallel velour upholstery, sunroof, adjustable headlight elevation and electric windows and mirrors. (Michael Dyas)

This cherished three-door Saab 900 XS was first registered in 1992, and is finished in an attractive Nocturne-Blue Metallic. It has had just one owner from new. To date, it has covered 163,000 miles on its original engine. (Michael Dyas)

Saab 900 Ruby (1992–1993)

Only 150 Ruby special editions were produced for the UK market. All were based on the three-door coupé and they featured the B201 series, sixteen-valve turbo engine with a red case engine control unit (ECU), delivering 185 bhp. The entire production run was painted in Ruby mica red metallic paint, with bespoke Ruby-painted bumpers front and rear, and Super Aero alloys with dark grey centres and polished aluminium rims. The special run was finished with standard body mouldings, rather than the Aero body kit. The interior had grey Buffalo leather, with all seat upholstery and door cards finished in a grey/red wool fabric supplied by Italian fashion company Ermenegildo Zegna. All 900 Ruby vehicles had cruise control, electric windows and mirrors, and electric sunroof.

This Saab 900 Ruby was first registered in 1993, and is one of 150 special-edition models produced for the UK market in the final year of production of the Saab 900. They were all fitted with the 185-bhp turbo 16S engine, and had Ruby-mica metallic-paint finish, leather seats with Zegna cloth inserts, cruise control, whale-tail rear spoilers, and front and rear bumpers finished in the body colour. (Richard Horner)

The Saab 900 Ruby was a fitting swansong to fifteen years' production of a superbly engineered car. This low-angle shot shows off the asymmetrical alloy wheels with grey centres and polished rims. (Mike Ironside)

This low-angle shot captures the stylish looks of the Saab 900 Ruby special edition well. None of the 150 Saab 900 Ruby special editions sold in the UK had body skirts. (Mike Ironside)

The badge on the hatchback gave no clue that the 900 Ruby was a special edition at all, with the car bearing the same badging as a standard 175-bhp Saab 900 turbo. (Mike Ironside)

This Saab 900 Ruby edition is seen when nearly new at a Saab rally in northern England, and is in totally original condition. (Richard Horner)

A view of the engine bay of a Saab 900 Ruby special edition. The Ruby was fitted with a red top-engine management unit, which gave an output of 185 bhp, 10 bhp more than the Saab 900 turbo S. It is seen on the left side of the wheel-arch. (Richard Horner)

Saab 900i Aero (1992–1993)

In the final year of Saab 900 production, Saab fitted a number of 900i three-door coupés with the distinctive grey Aero body kit fitted to the 900 S and 900 turbo S models, probably in order to use up stocks and attract buyers to the base 900i model. The 900i Aero was otherwise the same as a conventional 900i, including deep-velour seating, but featured an electric sunroof and rear rubber spoiler. Exact production figures are unknown, and most seemed to have been produced in either Black or Imola Red.

An immaculate Saab 900i Aero, first registered in 1992, is shown in Imola Red with the Anthracite-Grey body skirts. Except from the rear, where the 900i badge was plainly visible, it is hard to tell the difference between 900i Aero and Saab 900 turbo S models. (Richard Horner)

The 900i Aero was only produced in the 1992–3 model years, and featured velour upholstery, electric front windows and sunroof, asymmetric alloy wheels and grey Aero body skirts. To all intents and purposes, it passed as a 900 S or 900 turbo S Aero car, but without the performance! This example, finished in Black, also has the optional Saab bonnet-edge protector fitted. This was designed to resist stone chip damage to the outer front edge of the bonnet. It is also fitted with another dealer option, the clear headlight protector, designed to prevent chipping to headlight glass. (Alex Rankin)

Saab 900 Special Edition convertible (1993)

The final run of classic Saab 900 convertibles in 1993 was available in low- or high-pressure turbo forms in metallic Nova Black. Most featured grey asymmetric wheels with polished rims, as per the 900 Ruby. The 175-bhp, high-pressure turbo S car was fitted with cruise control and leather upholstery, and had a walnut instrument panel. Additionally, a small number of 1993 run-out convertibles featured a brand-new Saab body colour, Aubergine metallic.

A small run of 1993 model-year Saab 900 convertibles exported to the UK was finished in a new Saab colour, Aubergine Metallic. This is a 1993 Saab 900 turbo S in the attractive paint scheme, which is easy to mistake for Odoardo Grey. (Mark Gardiner)

Interior view of a 1993 Saab 900 S turbo, showing the walnut veneer dashboard, later-style padded steering wheel, revised glove box and sunroof securing points on the top rail of the windscreen. (Richard Horner)

89

This superb cherished Saab 900 S convertible in Nova Black Metallic was first registered in the UK in March 1993. (Richard Horner)

The immaculate Nova Black paint is complemented by an Anthracite-Grey body kit and Silver asymmetrical Super Aero alloy wheels. A small number of UK commemorative run-out convertibles had the same paint scheme with Graphite Grey Super Aeros and polished rims. (Richard Horner)

Saab Friction Tester (1979–1993)

Saab supplied a number of specially adapted 900 models, called Friction Testers, to airports around the world. They were used to measure the friction and rolling resistance of runways, especially in bad weather, to help advise pilots about safe landing points and braking distances. The boot area of a standard three-door car was heavily modified to accommodate an aeroplane-sized wheel, which was lowered onto the runway surface while the car was at speed, as engineers recorded data on specialised equipment inside the car. It is believed that a number are still in use around the world.

This bright-orange Saab Friction Tester from 1979 is clearly based on the Saab 900 EMS with its distinctive 'soccer-ball' alloy wheels. (Keith Long/SOC Archive)

This Swedish-registered Saab Friction Tester dates from around 1984 and shows the revised front grille and thicker side-body mouldings. (Keith Long/SOC Archive)

Technical data – 1988 model year

Dimensions
Overall length: 4,687–4,739 mm
Overall width: 1,690 mm
Overall height: 1,400–1,420 mm
Overall height, convertible: 2,250 mm
Track between front wheels on 5.5J x 15 H2 rims: 1,430 mm
Track between rear wheels on 5.5J x 15 H2 rims: 1,440 mm
Wheelbase: 2,517 mm
Turning circle: 11.2 m
Maximum weight fully laden: 1,600–1,760 mm
Fuel tank capacity: 63 litres

Interior
Volume of luggage compartment:
Combi coupe, parcel shelf fitted: 0.421 cu m (14.9 cu. feet)
Combi coupe, parcel shelf removed: 0.540 cu m (19.1 cu. feet)
Saloon: 0.408 cu m (14.4 cu. feet)
Convertible: 0.279 cu m (9.9 cu. feet)

Volume of luggage compartment, rear seat folded:
two-door and four-door models: 1.5 cu m (53 cu. feet)
three-door and five-door models: 1.6 cu m (56.5 cu. feet)

Length of luggage compartment, rear seat folded:
two-door and four-door models: 1,755 mm
three-door and five-door models: 1,835 mm

Engine
900, 900i and 900 turbo 8: Four-cylinder, four-stroke, single overhead camshaft engine
900 turbo 16: Four cylinder, four stroke, double-overhead camshaft engine

Cylinder bore: 90 mm
Stroke: 78 mm
Swept volume: 1,985 cu. cm
Idling speed: 800–900 r/min

Carburetted engine
Rating (DIN) 73 kW (100 hp) at 5,200 r/min
Torque (DIN) 163 Nm at 3,500 r/min
Carburettor: Pierburg 175 CDUS

Fuel injection engine
Rating (DIN) 87 kW (100 hp) at 5,500 r/min
Torque (DIN) 167 Nm at 3,000 r/min
Fuel injection system: BOSCH CI

Turbo 8 fuel-injected engine
Rating (DIN) 114 kW (155 hp) at 5,000 r/min
Torque (DIN) 240 Nm at 3,000 r/min
Fuel injection system: BOSCH CI
Turbocharger make: Garrett AiResearch

Turbo 16 fuel-injected engine
Rating (DIN) 129 kW (175 hp) at 5,300 r/min
Torque (DIN) 273 Nm at 3,000 r/min
Fuel injection system: BOSCH LH
Turbocharger make: Garrett AiResearch

Acknowledgements

My grateful thanks go to Peter Bäckström at the Saab Car Museum in Trollhättan, Sweden, and Mikael Maki at Valmet Automotive in Uusikaupunki, Finland, for their assistance in sourcing photos and information. In addition, thanks go to Alex Rankin of the 900 register of the Saab Owners Club of Great Britain (SOC), Keith Long, librarian/archivist of the SOC, and all Saab owners and SOC members who have supplied photographs of cars, who are duly credited in this book. My grateful thanks also go to Susan Bennett, who encouraged me to write this book.

Bibliography

Chatterton, Mark, *Saab: The Innovator* (1980)
Cole, Lance, *Saab 99 and 900: The Complete Story* (2001)
Cole, Lance, *Saab Cars* (2012)
Dymock, Eric, *Saab: Half a Century of Achievement* (1997)
Lindh, Björn-Erik, *The First 40 Years of Saab Cars* (1987)
Robson, Graham, *Saab Turbo* (1983)
Sjögren, Gunnar A., *The Saab Way* (1984)
Tunberg, Anders, *The Cars in the Saab Museum* (1989)

Further information about the Saab 900 and other models is available on the following Saab enthusiast websites:

www.saabplanet.com (Saab Planet)
www.saabworld.net (Saab World)
www.uksaabs.co.uk (UKSaabs)
www.saabklubben.se (Swedish Saab Club)
www.saabclub.fi (The Saab Club of Finland)
www.saabclub.nl (Saab Club Nederland)
www.saabclub.co.uk (Saab Owners Club of Great Britain)
www.saabclub.com (The Saab Club of North America)